EVERYTHING YOU NEED TO KNOW ABOUT

CONFRONTING XENOPHOBIA

SUSAN MEYER

Rosen
YA™
New York

Published in 2019 by The Rosen Publishing Group, Inc.
29 East 21st Street, New York, NY 10010

First Edition

Library of Congress Cataloging-in-Publication Data

Names: Meyer, Susan, 1986– author.
Title: Everything you need to know about confronting xenophobia / Susan Meyer.
Description: New York : Rosen Publishing, 2019 | Series: The need to know library | Includes bibliographical references and index. | Audience: Grades 7–12.
Identifiers: LCCN 2017045729| ISBN 9781508179177 (library bound) | ISBN 9781508179269 (pbk.)
Subjects: LCSH: Xenophobia—Juvenile literature.
Classification: LCC GN496 .M478 2019 | DDC 305.8—dc23
LC record available at https://lccn.loc.gov/2017045729

Manufactured in the United States of America

CONTENTS

INTRODUCTION

Our world is a diverse place full of many kinds of people. These people speak different languages, celebrate different holidays, believe in different religions, and live in different countries. People sometimes move to new countries to live. Usually people in the new countries they move to are welcoming and accepting of their different backgrounds and cultures. However, sometimes newcomers face fear and anger from their new neighbors. This fear and anger is known as xenophobia.

People who are xenophobic are hostile toward people from different backgrounds. They feel they have to defend their country from outsiders coming into it. They may do this by shouting at or taunting people who are different from them or people they see as outsiders. Their goal is to make people feel unwelcome. Xenophobia means an intense fear or hatred of foreigners, or people thought to have come from other countries. Unfortunately, xenophobia is not a new problem. It is one that has existed around the world and throughout human history.

In our modern times, we still haven't figured out how to get rid of xenophobia. You can still see examples of xenophobic speech and actions in the United States today. For example, in the summer of 2017, two Muslim teen girls were hanging out at a restaurant in

People's clothing can showcase their diverse beliefs. This woman is wearing a sari and has a bindi on her forehead. The bindi is often worn by Hindu women.

Hickory Hills, Illinois. An older white man took note of the scarves they wore on their heads as part of their faith. He began to yell at the girls and make insulting comments. While it can be easy to be intimidated by a xenophobic person, the girls were not afraid to confront him. They approached the table where he was eating and asked why he was yelling at them. The man told them they should go back to where they came from, and the girls explained to him that the United States was their home. As one of the two girls, Sawin Osman, would later tell Yahoo! News, "It's honestly very terrible and disgusting, especially the comment, 'If you don't like it, then just leave.' I mean I was born here. I was raised here. Leave to where?"

When they turned to walk away, the man began yelling curses after them, but they calmly exited the situation. The incident was recorded on cell phone video and posted on the internet. Ultimately, the teen girls looked like the responsible adults in the situation, and the xenophobic man appeared hateful and ignorant.

Confronting xenophobia is never easy. It takes bravery and strong convictions. But by confronting people who express xenophobic beliefs or standing up in the name of the people they try to make into outsiders, you support a culture of diversity that is an important part of keeping our communities safe and welcoming.

CHAPTER ONE

FEAR OF DIFFERENCES

When you see the word "xenophobia," you might think of other phobias you know. Phobias usually mean being very scared of a certain thing. For example, claustrophobia is the fear of being in tight spaces, and arachnophobia is the fear of spiders. Xenophobia is not quite the same. The definition of xenophobia is a fear of foreigners or those who seem foreign. This can mean people who come from other countries. It can also mean people who grew up in your country but look different or celebrate different cultures.

Unlike with other phobias, xenophobic people aren't just scared. They don't run away and hide from people who they believe are foreign. Instead, they go out of their way to try to intimidate them and make them feel like outsiders.

People who are xenophobic are called xenophobes. Xenophobes have strong beliefs about people who are different than they are. This fear and distrust of foreigners or those perceived to be foreign can lead xenophobes to lash out in angry and sometimes dangerous ways. Their beliefs may stem from how they were taught

People who are xenophobic are often used to fitting in. They tend to be skeptical of the motives of people who are from other places.

their whole lives, and their minds are not necessarily easy to change. However, that doesn't mean that those beliefs should go unchallenged. Learning to recognize and confront xenophobic people and xenophobic behavior is the only way to work toward helping both xenophobes and the people they target.

RACISM, XENOPHOBIA, AND DISCRIMINATION

You are likely familiar with the concept of racism and what it means to be racist. If so, you may think that racism seems very similar to xenophobia. While the two issues are related, they are not the same thing. Racism is defined as prejudice against a group because of their race and having the belief that one race is superior to other races. Race is simply a classification of humans based on physical characteristics. While racists are prejudiced against people because of their race, xenophobes are

WHAT'S IN A WORD?

The word "xenophobia" finds its roots in the language of the ancient Greeks. But that doesn't mean that the word was actually created by them. In ancient Greek, the word *phobos* means "fear." The word *xenos* can be translated as either "stranger" or "guest." The word "xenophobia" itself, despite its ancient roots, was coined much later. People used the Greek roots to create a word that meant what they needed it to. The word is thought to have first appeared in print with its modern meaning in 1903. This was many centuries after the civilization of the ancient Greeks had collapsed.

While the word itself may be more recent, the concept still dates back to early civilizations. Since the beginning of time, people have had trouble accepting people from outside their group, country, or civilization. It just took a while to give that feeling the official name we know today.

prejudiced against people because of their nationality or where they come from.

While the two ideas are different, they do share many similarities. Racism and xenophobia prop each other up and share similar methods of prejudice and hate speech. Many people who are xenophobic are also racist, and vice versa. Both xenophobia and racism operate on the same basis of profiling people and making negative assumptions about them based on those profiles. This means both xenophobes and racists look at the actions of one person from a group and apply those actions to the whole group. Xenophobic people may also see a person's race as a sign that they are an outsider and from another country.

Discrimination is also not quite the same thing as xenophobia, although people who are xenophobic do often discriminate against people they feel are different from them. Discrimination means treating people differently because of their race, gender, sexual orientation, culture, religion, or ethnicity. When people discriminate they treat all individuals from a group differently just because they are part of that group. For example, in

The more you get to know people from other places and of other backgrounds, the more you understand that they are individuals and can't be reduced to stereotypes.

the 1950s, discrimination was a regular practice in the United States. Black Americans weren't allowed to sit on certain bus seats, drink from certain water fountains, or go to certain schools simply because they were black.

Xenophobes may discriminate against people based on their nationality or their ethnicity. Xenophobic discrimination can be very obvious, like not letting people who appear to be from a certain country shop at a store or yelling at them to leave a public place. It can also be more subtle. For example, some studies show that people with foreign-sounding last names on their résumés get fewer interviews for jobs even if they have similar skills and experience. These types of discrimination are harder to prove. The person doing the discriminating might not even be aware of their own subtle bias. Nevertheless, both subtle and obvious forms of discrimination can make it more difficult for people who experience them.

THE LINK BETWEEN XENOPHOBIA AND IMMIGRATION

People do not always spend their whole lives in the country where they were born. When a person enters a new country, they are immigrating. People have many reasons for immigrating. Some are leaving their home country when it is unsafe because of war or environmental conditions. Others wish to move to a country that has better job opportunities or a better quality of life. Some also immigrate in order to reunite with family members who have already moved. You may have heard that the United States is a nation built by immigrants. This is because, other than the Native Americans who lived here for thousands of years, most of the population is descended from people who came from other countries within the last five hundred years.

Most countries have an immigration policy. An immigration policy says who can come into a country and how long they can stay. It also establishes things like whether they can work in the country. Not everyone agrees on what their country's immigration policy should be. Some people believe that the United States should have a more open immigration policy. They

These protesters in West Palm Beach, Florida, are speaking out for stronger immigration policies. They believe these policies will help American workers find better jobs.

believe that immigrants add many benefits to the country. They may also be sympathetic to people who want to immigrate because their own country is unsafe or unstable. Other people believe that the United States should close and guard its borders and let fewer people in. These people feel that there are too many people already and that strong borders keep the country safe.

Issues of immigration and xenophobia are often linked. There are two sides to the immigration debate and both have valid arguments. However, people who oppose immigration sometimes do so because of xenophobic biases. They may fear immigrants and what they bring to the country. They may also treat all immigrants, even those who live in this country legally, as if they have illegally crossed the border.

WHY SO SCARED?

There are a number of reasons that xenophobic people are scared of foreigners. One is the fear that foreigners will take their jobs. This is why xenophobia is often particularly bad in times of economic crisis. When people are poor and struggling to care for their families, they may become scared about their future and angry about their situation. Being scared and angry at your circumstances is frustrating. Some people redirect those emotions toward other people. They look for someone to blame for their circumstances. There is a long history of blaming foreigners or outsiders for problems. The logic goes that if there were fewer people, there would be more jobs available. One way to limit the number of people competing for jobs is to limit the number of people coming into the country. In reality, immigrants often help create jobs. More people buying products creates a high demand for goods and services. Immigrants are also twice as likely to start a business as native-born citizens. These businesses can then hire more workers, creating new jobs.

Another fear that fuels xenophobia is that immigrants take resources away from native-born citizens. People with these concerns often believe that most people they see who appear to be from other countries are there illegally. All citizens of a country have to pay a portion

Many immigrants—such as this grocery owner—improve the economy by starting their own businesses and hiring workers.

of their income as tax. This helps the government to function and to pay for services that help its citizens. If people don't pay taxes to support the country, then they don't deserve to be there, is the belief. However, immigrants actually pay between $90 and $140 billion in US taxes each year. A 2012 study found that even undocumented immigrants in the United States paid almost $12 billion in taxes in that year. All people who live in the United States, regardless of where they came from or how long they have lived here, spend money and make purchases. This helps fuel the economy.

Some people also fear that immigrants are dangerous and bring more crime with them. This is often centered around people of certain religions. Islamophobia is a form of xenophobia in which the people targeted are those who follow the religion of Islam. People who follow Islam are also known as Muslims. People who are Islamophobes think that because some terrorist attacks have been committed by Muslims all Muslims are potentially dangerous. They see the actions of a few individuals and apply them to the whole group.

MYTHS AND FACTS

MYTH: Foreigners steal jobs from American citizens.

FACT: In 2016, a 550-page report was compiled by fourteen leading economists. The report concluded that there were "little to no negative effects on overall wages and employment of native-born workers in the longer term" as a result of immigration.

MYTH: There are too many immigrants. They're taking over our country.

FACT: It's true that there are more immigrants living in the United States than ever before but only because the total population is greater than ever before. In fact, the percentage of immigrants is about the same as it has been for most of our history: around 15 percent.

MYTH: Immigrants cause more crime and make cities unsafe.

FACT: Studies consistently show that immigrants are less likely to be incarcerated than native-born citizens. Also, when the number of people coming to the United States increased sharply between 1990 and 2010, the amount of violent crime also decreased in the country.

CHAPTER TWO

XENOPHOBIA AROUND THE WORLD

P eople fearing foreigners and trying to make them feel like outsiders is nothing new. Throughout human history, different groups of people have always had trouble getting along with each other.

In truth, people are not so different from one another. We may have different cultural backgrounds and beliefs. We might have slightly different skin tones or wear different clothes. However, we are all part of the same species, *Homo sapiens*. So why would we go out of our way to seek out differences and try to exclude others?

One reason is because civilizations often define themselves by identifying who is a member of the civilization and who is not. As civilizations begin to form, they focus on common traits to keep people working together toward common goals. Early humans joined together in small groups that gradually grew larger and broke off into different groups. To feel connected as a tribe or civilization, people instinctively clung to the people near them. This trend has continued long after we moved from these early civilizations. Now we live in countries with borders, and there is an even more strict division between one group and another.

BARBARIANS

When you hear the word "barbarian," you probably think of someone who is bloodthirsty and uncivilized. The word comes from the ancient Greek word *barbaros*, which the Greeks used to describe people who did not speak Greek. The ancient Romans later adopted the term to refer to many of the people they conquered in their quest to expand their empire. They saw

This piece of Roman art from 250 CE shows a battle between the Romans and the Goths. The Romans often categorized the people they conquered as bloodthirsty barbarians.

these people as the enemy. They ate different food than the Romans, and they had different customs. Interestingly, in this case, it was the Romans who were the foreigners. They were coming into people's territories to expand their empire. They quickly took control and made the land their own. Those who didn't join their culture were treated poorly and sometimes enslaved.

By characterizing the people they conquered as barbarians, the Romans taught their own people that the conquered people were scary and deserved to be conquered. Teaching people to fear people who are different from them is the foundation of xenophobia. Fear is a powerful emotion and can make people behave toward their fellow humans in truly unthinkable aways.

XENOPHOBIA DURING WORLD WAR II

Jumping forward in history, some of the most clear-cut cases of xenophobia took place during World War II, one of the largest conflicts in modern history. Leading up to World War II, the people of Germany faced many social and economic problems. Some of the problems were a result of World War I, which had occurred several years earlier. People were looking for someone to blame. The German leader Adolf Hitler rose to power by blaming Germany's problems on foreigners. He particularly blamed Jewish people. The German people were angry, scared, and worried about the future. Hitler used this atmosphere to his advantage and soon had control of much of Europe. He used this power to imprison and kill people who were considered foreign, especially Jewish people.

Jews were herded into certain parts of cities called ghettos where they were forced to live in tight quarters without much food. They were also sent to work camps and forced to perform hard labor without any pay. Ultimately, most were sent to concentration camps where they were deprived of food, separated from their families, forced to work, and eventually killed. These events are known as the Holocaust. More than six million Jewish people lost their lives in the Holocaust, as did a smaller number of Roma, gay people, and political opponents of the Nazi government that ruled Germany

This photo shows men in a barracks at a Japanese internment camp in California. These men were forced to live there because they were of Japanese origin, even though many were American citizens.

at the time. The Holocaust is proof that xenophobia can have horrifyingly tragic consequences.

The Holocaust was not the only example of xenophobia during World War II. In the United States, there were also strong xenophobic feelings during this time. One of the countries that the United States was at war with was Japan. Many Japanese Americans were robbed of their basic rights during this time. These were people who had emigrated from Japan and chose to call the United States home. More than half of them were legal United States citizens. They were taken from their homes and forced to move to relocation camps. This happened because Americans feared the Japanese and lashed out at Japanese Americans simply because they were of Japanese descent.

MODERN EXAMPLES OF XENOPHOBIA AROUND THE WORLD

Xenophobia continues to plague society today. There are a number of instances of people showing a lack of tolerance to those they view as outsiders. Not all of these situations are as serious as millions of people being killed, but all contribute to a culture of distrust and hate that can ultimately lead to larger events.

The Southeast Asian country Malaysia has serious issues with xenophobia. Most of the prejudice is toward people from Bangladesh who come to Malaysia for work. In 2014, the state of Penang in Malaysia decided that foreign cooks would be forbidden from

These foreign nationals in South Africa are taking their belongings and quickly heading to a bus back to Zimbabwe. They are hoping to escape xenophobic attacks against people from Zimbabwe.

making and selling local cuisine. The vast majority of local Malaysians agreed with the law. They didn't see it as unfair that some food sellers would have to change what they sold or risk losing their business, just because they were not born in Malaysia.

South Africa has a long history of racism and xenophobia. For much of the twentieth century, black South Africans had very few rights and couldn't even vote in their own country. In 2015, there were a number of xenophobic attacks against workers who migrated from South Africa's neighbor to the north, Zimbabwe.

South Africans with xenophobic feelings believed that people from Zimbabwe and other foreigners were taking their scarce resources. These attacks took many forms. In some cases, foreigners living in South Africa were driven from their homes and villages. In other cases, their businesses were set on fire. The problem was not only limited to a handful of citizens, but also

IS XENOPHOBIA ON THE RISE?

In 2016 and 2017, the United States saw an increase in xenophobic language. Many people spoke out against allowing immigrants to enter the country and argued that those already there should be sent away. Even the president of the United States, Donald Trump, sometimes described immigrants as "gang members" or "drug dealers" or "rapists." These are powerful words intended to make people afraid.

When people hear these words used to characterize immigrants, especially from the mouth of a powerful leader, it can make them more nervous about immigrants. They may doubt their safety if immigrants are allowed into the country. People who oppose President Trump believe that his rhetoric is xenophobic and that it is causing more xenophobia in America. People who support President Trump believe he is making our country stronger and safer. Do you think President Donald Trump is causing the United States to be more xenophobic? Research both sides of the issue to help you make an informed decision.

high reaching political figures who fanned the flames. In 2015, a Zulu king named Goodwill Zwelithini publicly said that foreigners should go back to their home countries because they were creating a burden on South Africa. After his remarks, attacks against foreigners only increased.

In the United States, there are also issues with xenophobia. The United States was largely built by immigrants. And yet throughout its history, people arriving from countries ranging from Italy and Ireland to India and China have all faced discrimination from people already living there. In some cases, this fear stemmed from the belief that foreign workers would steal American jobs. In other cases, the fear came from the idea that the immigrants would make the country less safe. Some even believe that people who weren't born in the United States can't contribute to the country in the same way as those that were.

Now that you know a little about the past and current history of xenophobia, it's important to consider why it is a bad thing. How does it affect both the people who are targeted with xenophobic rhetoric and even the people doing the targeting?

CHAPTER THREE

THE CONSEQUENCES OF XENOPHOBIA

I magine you move to a new town or school. You want people to like you, and you want to fit into the rules of the place you've moved. But at the same time, you like things about your old school or your old town. You don't want to lose those parts of your identity. You hope that your new classmates and community members will welcome you and be happy you're there. But what if they don't? If people went out of their way to remind you that you don't belong and that you're different, you wouldn't be comfortable there. This would especially be the case if this treatment continued long after you felt like you were a true member of the new community.

Xenophobia feels like this but on a much larger scale because people may have come from much farther away. People may have left their previous homes for any number of reasons. In some cases, they might have been leaving behind problems such as war or food shortages. In other cases, they might have traveled to find better jobs to help support their families. Others might have moved to be closer to loved ones. Whatever the reason, they want to make a home in their new country. But making a home in

People from different backgrounds can provide a wealth of new perspectives. Try starting a conversation with someone who comes from a different culture or religious group.

a new country doesn't mean completely changing one's identity. What makes the United States such a wonderful and diverse place is that it celebrates people from all cultures. The country gains richness by being multicultural, or made up of many cultures, instead of forcing everyone to be the same.

People who are xenophobic fail to see the value in people from different cultures and experiences. Instead, they only see difference as a negative thing. They don't understand that people can call a country their home while still keeping parts of other cultures and religions in their identities.

WHO ARE THE TARGETS OF XENOPHOBIA?

The most likely targets of xenophobia are people who look different or have visual clues to their cultural identity. After all, racism and xenophobia often go hand in hand because xenophobic people use race as a signal that someone is from a different place. People who dress differently because of their culture or religion are often targets of xenophobia. Muslim women are often targeted for wearing a hijab, or headscarf. This garment is traditionally worn by Muslim women as a sign of their faith.

If you have been the target of an angry rant because of the way you look or someone has made you feel like

The hijab, like the one worn by this young woman, is a garment that covers the head and neck. Muslim women wear it as a symbol of modesty.

you don't belong, then you know what xenophobia feels like. It is incredibly alienating. The goal is to isolate you and make you feel like you aren't welcome. It also might not make you have very warm feelings toward your new country. Living in a place that doesn't accept you for who you are makes it harder for you to love your new country and truly be happy there.

NICK VALENCIA'S STORY

In a CNN story, a third-generation Mexican American man named Nick Valencia told of being yelled at by a woman at a music festival in Atlanta, Georgia. He had just struck up a conversation with strangers in line who happened to be from Mexico City, and he was enjoying getting to speak Spanish with them. Then, as Nick describes, a woman started shouting at them.

Nick recalls: "'Go home!' she yelled at me. 'Why don't you go back home to Mexico before you ruin this country like you ruined your own!'" Nick was shocked because he has lived his whole life in the United States, and it is the only home he has ever known. "Evidently, to some the brown color of my skin means I'm not even American."

In the moment, Nick was so shocked he didn't know what to say. Luckily, he didn't have to say anything. The crowd around him was shocked, too, and quickly came to his defense, telling the woman to leave. Confronting xenophobia is important because it reminds the target that he or she is not alone, and the community is, in fact, behind the victim.

WHAT DOES XENOPHOBIA LOOK LIKE?

Xenophobia appears in a number of ways. Sometimes it is very obvious and loud. People may say very ugly things to each other. They may use coarse language or stereotypes. They could yell insults at a person they want to intimidate or make feel like an outsider. However, not all xenophobic language is shouted in angry slurs at individuals. It doesn't always involve telling people directly to go back to where they came from. There are more subtle ways that xenophobia is present in our language. Here are three phrases that you might not realize are xenophobic:

- "But where are you really from?" It's always fine to ask people where they are from. However, if you are asking because you think they are a different nationality and you want to know their background, it can be offensive to press the question. If they tell you they are from the United States, that is where they are from. Accept their identity.
- "We need to defend our borders." While it's understandable for a country and the people in it to want to stay safe from attacks, when used to talk about immigrants, this statement implies that people— who may be fleeing their own countries for their own safety—are a threat just by existing. A border is a line on the map. It doesn't define the quality of the people on either side of it. There are both good and bad people on both sides of any border.

Sometimes people who come from the same country may choose to converse in their native language. Xenophobic people sometimes take offense when people don't speak English in front of them.

- "People should learn to speak English!" While English is the most common spoken language in the United States, the country does not have an official language. By telling people they should learn English, people are expressing that the language other people are speaking keeps them from belonging in this country. In reality, whether you choose to speak English or not, you can still be welcome in the United States.

CHAPTER FOUR

TAKING A STAND AGAINST XENOPHOBIA

N ow that you understand a little more about what xenophobia is and how it appears in our everyday language and culture, you may wonder what you can do to stop it. The most important thing to do is to recognize xenophobia when you see it happening and to stand up to the person causing it. This is easier said than done. It may take some practice.

STEPS TO CONFRONTING XENOPHOBIA

There are two types of xenophobia-related scenarios that you are most likely to encounter in your school or community. The first is when you see someone being attacked by a xenophobic person or persons. Here is an example: You are sitting in a local diner enjoying a meal with your friends. There is a family speaking in Spanish at the next table. A man walks by their table and starts to get very agitated. He begins yelling at the family that they should speak English because they're in America. He tells them if they don't want to speak

English they should go back to Mexico. The family calmly asks him to leave them alone, but he keeps yelling at them. What do you do?

In cases when someone is being personally attacked, it is a good opportunity to step in and confront the attacker. This is true both if you are defending someone being attacked or if you are the person being attacked. These attacks tend to be verbal rather than physical. If an attack is physical, go find an adult to help right away. If the attack is verbal, and you feel safe doing so, you can stand up to defend the targeted individuals. In the example in the restaurant, you would want to address the xenophobic person. Tell them: "This family has just

If you witness someone being the target of a xenophobic attack, one of the best ways to help is to support the attacked person and let him or her know he or she is not alone.

as much of a right to be here as you or I do. Please leave them alone to enjoy their dinner." If the person begins yelling at you or doesn't back down from the situation, try to enlist the help of others. In the restaurant example, consider looking for a person who works there or a manager. Or if the incident occurred at school, find a teacher or a principal. While xenophobes can be very loud and hard to ignore, they do not represent the majority of people. It is usually not hard to find someone else who disagrees with them nearby.

The goal in these types of situations is to de-escalate the situation as best you can. The most important thing is for the people who were being attacked to feel safe and to know that there are people on their side. Nothing can make people feel more alone than if someone attacks them and nobody stands up to say the attacker is wrong. This might make victims think that everyone around feels the same way. You can help them by showing that not everyone feels that they don't belong. Once the immediate situation is over, offer support. Tell them that the person who was attacking is part of a small minority of people who feel that way. These simple words can help people feel less alone and less like they are not a valued part of a country they may have called home for only a few years or for their whole lives.

The second type of situation you may encounter is when people say something xenophobic in your presence. They may be repeating something they have heard on the news or something a friend has told them. Xenophobia isn't always as obvious as someone yelling or

Xenophobia doesn't just happen in person; it is also a huge problem online. Unfortunately xenophobic comments are common online.

threatening another person. The roots of xenophobia in a culture can be more subtle, and these roots can run deep. As an example of this type of situation, imagine that you're sitting in the cafeteria with your friends. One of your friends makes a joke about people from another country or culture. You realize the joke is xenophobic. How do you respond? Another example of this type of situation is if you see a friend post something xenophobic on a social media platform. If the comment is online, it may be better to reach out to your friend in person or send them a direct message rather than commenting on the post. Texts can be easy for someone to take the wrong way. People may become defensive, and online comment threads can quickly turn mean and unproductive.

While your main goal in the first type of situation was to help the person targeted, in the second type there may be an opportunity for learning. It can be uncomfortable to tell friends that what they said is offensive, but it is also an

XENOPHOBIA ONLINE

Xenophobia is too often found online. You might see it in the comments section of a news article. Some online newspapers and magazines have even closed their comments sections to prevent people from saying offensive things. You might also see it on social media. Facebook and Twitter are places where people like to share their beliefs or debate about political issues. Some of their statements and beliefs may be xenophobic or racist. Online games are also a hotbed of xenophobic comments. The competitive spirit and "trash talk" can easily turn nasty and discriminatory.

Why are people more likely to say racist or xenophobic things online? It is often for the same reason that cyberbullying is sadly very common. With a greater distance between the person making the comment and the person receiving the comment, there is a loss of empathy, and people have more trouble putting themselves in someone else's shoes.

important part of confronting xenophobia. In these types of situations, be casual, but direct. Don't laugh at the joke or remark. Tell the friend who made the xenophobic joke or comment that it is offensive and hurtful to people. If the comment your friend made was based on incorrect facts, provide him or her with the correct information. Try to be friendly and encouraging in your explanation. You want to help your friends learn without making them feel attacked.

SAFETY PLANNING WHEN CHALLENGING A XENOPHOBIC PERSON

While it is worthwhile to challenge xenophobic beliefs when you see them occurring, don't do so at the risk of your own safety. Xenophobic people are often angry. Usually they will just express themselves through loud, angry words. However, sometimes this anger can lead them to violent actions.

In May 2017, a man named Jeremy Joseph Christian started yelling anti-Muslim slurs at two teenage girls on a train in Portland, Oregon. He told the young women to "go back to Saudi Arabia" and made many more extremely offensive statements. The two girls tried to remove themselves from the situation by moving to another part of the train. Three brave men, Ricky John Best, Taliesin Myrddin Namkai-Meche, and Micah David-Cole Fletcher moved between Christian and the girls. They tried to calm Christian down and de-escalate the situation. They suggested he get off the train. Christian pulled out a knife and attacked the three men. He ended up killing Best and Namkai-Meche and injuring Fletcher. Two men lost their lives because they tried to do the right thing and defend two innocent girls from being verbally attacked by a xenophobic person.

Situations like what occurred in Portland are rare. Most xenophobic people you encounter will not be physically violent. That said, it is important to be aware that some people may be unstable. Use good

This memorial remembers the heroism of Taliesin Myrddin Namkai-Meche and Ricky Best. The men were fatally stabbed in Portland, Oregon, while trying to stop a xenophobic attack on two teen girls.

judgement before getting involved, even if you are in a public place with many people around. If someone shows signs of being unstable, has a weapon, or threatens you physically in any way, leave the situation immediately and find someone to call the police. It is good to defend people who are being targeted because of their religion, culture, or ethnicity but not at the expense of your own safety. In these cases, your best option for helping is to find an adult to help.

UNDERSTANDING XENOPHOBIC FEELINGS WITHIN YOURSELF

Knowing xenophobic language is unfriendly

You may realize that some of the ideas you have grown up with or heard on TV are actually xenophobic. Take the time to process how you feel about these ideas.

and alienating to those who are forced to experience it is one thing. It can be easy to see that language in other people, especially when it is obvious, like people shouting at others in a public place. However, it isn't always so easy to recognize the more subtle xenophobic ideas that exist in our culture. It can be even harder to recognize them in your own thoughts and actions. It's important to think about and be aware of your own prejudices so that you can work through them. If you realize that something you have said is xenophobic, apologize for your words and reslove to avoid that kind of comment in the future.

Learning the facts about xenophobia can help you understand these feelings and work past them. One tool to help you do this is to focus on empathy. Empathy means having the ability to feel someone else's pain or to see the world from someone else's point of view. Empathy helps us to see the humanity in other people and understand where they might be coming from. For example, if a part of you wonders why people who live in the United States shouldn't be forced to learn English, try to imagine what it would be like to be in their shoes. If you have ever tried to learn a second language, you may know how difficult it is. Even if you only speak English, you likely know it is a complicated language. It can take a long time to learn all the rules. Being empathetic means seeing how it might be hard for people moving here to pick up English quickly. It also means understanding that even if they do learn English, they might still enjoy speaking their original language sometimes. It may be easier for them to fully express themselves in their native tongue.

If you or a friend ever have a thought or make a comment that may be subtly xenophobic, take a moment to put yourself in the shoes of an immigrant. Appreciate the person's struggles as a fellow human being. How would you feel if you were in their position? How might you feel if you had to face these subtle comments every day? Taking a moment to go through this process can go a long way toward stamping out xenophobia.

10 QUESTIONS TO ASK A TEACHER

1. What should I do when I hear a student say something xenophobic to another student?
2. What if the xenophobic person is an adult?
3. If I am the target of xenophobic hate speech, how should I safely remove myself from the situation?
4. Where can I go for help if I feel uncomfortable or attacked at school?
5. What type of language is considered xenophobic?
6. Other than language, what actions and attitudes are xenophobic?
7. Where can I learn more about xenophobia and current immigration debates?
8. How can I learn more about students from other cultures?
9. How can I help encourage a diverse, welcoming environment in our school?
10. What clubs or groups can I join that support people from other countries, cultures, or religions?

CHAPTER FIVE

CELEBRATING DIVERSITY

Xenophobia isn't just wrong because it makes people feel like outsiders in their home. It is also wrong because it tries to make people give up parts of their identity to fit in. When that happens, everyone loses because we end up having a less diverse culture. Immigrants coming to the United States have brought with them festivals, foods, ideas, and languages that contribute to what makes the country great today.

In fact, many icons that we may consider uniquely American were actually contributed by immigrants. The White House in Washington, DC, was designed by a man who emigrated from Ireland in the eighteenth century. The Brooklyn Bridge in New York City was also designed by an immigrant—a man named John Augustus Roebling who moved to the United States from Germany. Hot dogs, now an American staple, weren't first created here. Frankfurters were first brought to the United States by a German immigrant who opened the first hot dog stand in Coney Island in New York. Even the song "God Bless

Irving Berlin was a singer and songwriter who wrote many classic songs, including "God Bless America." He was also an immigrant who came to the United States at the age of five.

America" was written by a Jewish immigrant from what is now the country of Belarus.

So why don't Americans always welcome new people and their ideas? One way to help confront xenophobia is to be proactive. Stop xenophobic language and feelings before they start. Here are some ways you can not only confront xenophobia but encourage a more diverse and welcoming environment in your community.

SUPPORTING A DIVERSE COMMUNITY

One of the reasons xenophobia exists is because people look for differences instead of similarities. They look at someone who may have come from a different place or who has a different cultural background and see a stranger. They don't see another human who simply has other experiences to share. And in the process, it's easy to miss out on the richness of those experiences.

To help support a diverse community, consider ways you can get outside your own worldview. If your school has multicultural or diversity clubs that you can join, consider checking them out. It's also a good idea to see what types of events are available in your community. Local mosques, churches, or community groups often hold cultural events throughout the year that are open to the public. You may be able to find information about these opportunities by searching online, visiting your local library, or asking a teacher for help. If you find an event that sounds interesting, encourage your friends to join you and help spread the word. The more

Having friends from different backgrounds expands your worldview. Studies show it is also key to combating xenophobia.

you and other members of your community learn and appreciate other cultures, the easier it is to be empathetic to the struggles that people from other cultures may face.

Studies show that empathy and cross-cultural friendships are some of the best ways to combat xenophobic views and reduce prejudices. In other words, if people have a friend from a different culture, they will be more likely to see people from that culture—and people from other cultures in general—as fellow humans who are worthy of concern and kindness.

STAY INFORMED

Another way you can both support diversity and combat xenophobia in your community is to

To expand your worldview, see if there are immigrant support groups or cultural groups in your community that have activities you can join.

always keep learning and shaping your ideas. If there are not a lot of immigrants or people from other cultural backgrounds in your immediate community, that doesn't mean you can't seek out more knowledge and understanding about them. Read their histories and understand some of the things they might be struggling with. Some of these things might be scary or very different from your own life, and some of their struggles might be similar. Another way you can seek out friendships with people who are different from you is to get an online pen pal. There are secure groups that can help you connect with kids your age from other countries who are looking to make cross-cultural friendships. Remember to use a secure, recognized pen pal group, and be careful when talking to strangers online. Ask a parent or teacher to help you find a group online that supports safe, cross-cultural chats.

You can also read about other cultures and other countries online to help you overcome stereotypes. This will give you more information to share when correcting someone who is making a xenophobic comment based on incorrect information. You can pay particularly close attention to your town or city. Research your town to learn what the demographics are. Find out what kinds of people call your city home. What you learn may surprise you. It will also give you opportunities for more research and to learn more about the place you call home. For example, if you find out your town has a large population of immigrants from a certain country, you may want to read more about that country to help you learn about these fellow members of your town.

Another way to be informed is to keep up with current events. It is a good idea to be aware of the news. There is a lot of information in the media and on the internet. Some posts and articles are more accurate than others. Being able to read multiple sources and decide what is true and what you believe is an important part of media literacy. A teacher can help you learn to recognize reliable news sources. You can read both sides of the immigration debate to learn the arguments that each side makes. You can also stay up to date on the most current immigration policies. You don't have to limit yourself to national news. You can also read about

WORLDMOSAIC

While xenophobia is a problem on a huge scale, small acts started by a single person can grow to make a big difference. For example, in April 2016, University of Alberta student Jeremiah Ellis decided to start a campaign to combat Islamophobia. For his campaign, Ellis talked to the mayor of the town of Edmonton, Alberta, where he lived and went to school. A few days later, the mayor made a post on social media holding up a sign with #WorldMosaic. His sign also stated that "Islamophobia has no place in Edmonton."

Soon, other mayors in towns around Canada were posting signs using the same hashtag. And after that, it spread from Canada to the United States, Australia, and New Zealand. Ellis was proud to see so many local, national, and world leaders supporting the message, saying "[They've] been supporting ... the fact this idea that diversity is our strength isn't just a Canadian value." Diversity is a strength of many countries, and sometimes it's great to spread the word that diversity and tolerance should be embraced.

xenophobia in other countries and how people there are dealing with it.

Xenophobia is an unfortunate part of human society. For as long as humans have gathered together into groups, we have also excluded people from those groups. But it doesn't have to be that way. Recognizing

These demonstrators gathered in January 2017 at JFK Airport in New York City to protest President Donald Trump's executive order banning immigrants from predominantly Muslim countries.

that we are all human and have more similarities than differences can help eliminate xenophobia from our world. Then we can allow those differences to be a thing for celebration, not something that keeps us apart.

Once you have a better understanding of what xenophobia is and how to recognize it, you'll be better prepared to confront it. Standing up to xenophobic people isn't easy. It takes bravery. But you should now feel empowered that you can take on xenophobia and help stamp it out of your community. You are armed with the knowledge and tools you need to help build a better world in which people are not made to feel like outsiders in the country they call home.

barbarians People who lack culture or are uncivilized.

bias A personal viewpoint that skews one's understanding of a topic or situation.

civilization A group of people living together who share the same culture.

demographics The statistics measuing the mix of people who make up the population in an area.

diverse Made up of many different parts.

empire A group of several countries or civilizations held together under the authority of one country or civilization.

foreign Of or from a country that is different from one's own.

garment A piece of clothing.

ghetto During World War II, a small, cramped, undesirable part of a city where certain people were forced to live.

immigrate To move to a country.

incarcerated Serving time in prison.

instinctively Based on habitual or inborn habit rather than thought.

intimidate To attempt to scare someone or make them feel unsafe.

Islamophobia The fear or hatred of people who follow the religion Islam.

native tongue The first language that a person speaks.

phobia An irrational fear of something.

prejudice An opinion about a group of people that is not based on fact.

proactive Causing something to happen rather than waiting for it to happen.

racism Believing that one's race is superior to people of other races.

résumé A summary of a person's work experience that is used to help them get a job.

species A specific kind of living thing. All human beings are the same species.

undocumented Referring to a person who is in a country without the legal documents saying he or she can be there.

Canadian Council for Refugees
6839 Drolet #301
Montréal, QC H2S 2T1
Canada
(514) 277-7223
Website: http://ccrweb.ca/en
Facebook and Twitter: @ccrweb
The Canadian Council for Refugees is a national non-
    profit organization dedicated to protecting the rights
    of refugees and vulnerable immigrants in Canada
    and around the world.

Human Rights First
333 Seventh Avenue, 13th Floor
New York, NY 10001
(212) 845-5200
Website: http://www.humanrightsfirst.org
Facebook: @humanrightsfirst
Twitter: @humanrights1st
Human Rights First is a nonprofit, nonpartisan interna-
    tional organization focused on the rights of all
    people. One of their many projects involved creating
    a blueprint for ending xenophobic violence.

National Council of Canadian Muslims (NCCM)
PO Box 13219
Ottawa, ON K2K 1X4

Canada
(866) 524-0004
Website: https://www.nccm.ca
Facebook: @NCCMuslims
Twitter: @nccm
The National Council of Canadian Muslims is an inde-
pendent, nonprofit organization that is devoted to
challenging xenophobia and particularly Islamophobia by protecting the rights of Canadian Muslims.

National Immigration Law Center (NILC)
3450 Wilshire Boulevard, #108–62
Los Angeles, CA 90010
(213) 639-3900
Website: https://www.nilc.org
Facebook: @NationalImmigrationLawCenter
Twitter: @NILC_org
The National Immigration Law Center is an organization
based in the United States dedicated specifically to
defending and advancing the rights of immigrants
who have low incomes.

The Office of the United Nations High Commissioner for
Refugees (UNHCR)
Case Postale 2500
CH-1211 Genève 2 Dépôt
Switzerland
+41 22 739 8111
Website: http://www.unhcr.org
Facebook: @UNHCR

Twitter: @Refugees

Also known as the UN Refugee Agency, the UNHCR is a global organization dedicated to saving lives, protecting rights, and improving the future for refugees and people without a home country. Since 2009, they have worked to help combat xenophobic violence in South Africa.

The Young Center
6020 South University Avenue
Chicago, IL 60637
(773) 702-9560
Website: http://theyoungcenter.org
Facebook and Twitter: @TheYoungCenter

This organization works to provide advocacy for the children of immigrants as they often struggle when facing the immigration system alone.

FOR FURTHER READING

Bailey, Rachel A. *The Japanese Internment Camps: A History Perspectives Books.* Ann Arbor, MI: Cherry Lake Publishing, 2014.

Baker, Brynn. *Life in America: Comparing Immigrant Experiences.* Mankato, MN: Capstone Press, 2015.

Dismondy, Maria, Nancy Day, and Donna Farrell. *Chocolate Milk, Por Favor: Celebrating Diversity with Empathy.* Dearborn, MI; First Publishing, 2015.

Herman, Gail, and Jerry Hoare. *What Was the Holocaust?* New York, NY: Penguin Young Readers, 2018.

Howell, Sara. *Famous Immigrants and Their Stories.* New York, NY: Rosen Publishing Group, 2014.

Hughes, Langston. *I, Too, Am America.* New York, NY: Simon & Schuster, 2012.

Iyer, Deepa. *We Too Sing America: South Asian, Arab, Muslim, and Sikh Immigrants Shape Our Multiracial Future.* New York, NY: New Press, 2015.

McDonald, James, and Rebecca McDonald. *Do I Look Odd to You: A Multicultural Children's Book About Embracing Diversity.* Salem, OR: House of Lore Publishing, 2015.

Ringgold, Faith. *We Came to America.* New York, NY: Penguin Random House, 2016.

Steele, Philip. *The Holocaust: The Origins, Events, and Remarkable Tales of Survival.* New York, NY: Scholastic Nonfiction, 2016.

Cashdan, Elizabeth. "Ethnocentrism and Xenophobia: A Cross-Cultural Study." *Current Anthropology* 42.5 (2001): 760–764.

Herf, Jeffrey. *The Jewish Enemy: Nazi Propaganda During World War II and the Holocaust.* Cambridge, MA: Belknap Press of Harvard University Press, 2006.

Llamas, Liliana. "10 Uniquely American Things Created by Immigrants." NBC Latino, July 21, 2013. http://nbclatino.com/2013/07/21/10-uniquely-american-things-created-by-immigrants.

"Man Berates Muslim Girls at Suburban Restaurant." CBS Chicago, June 6, 2017. http://chicago.cbslocal.com/2017/06/06/muslim-girls-verbally-abused-restaurant.

Novick, Peter. *The Holocaust in American Life.* New York, NY: Houghton Mifflin Harcourt, 2000.

Nyamnjoh, Francis B. *Insiders and Outsiders: Citizenship and Xenophobia in Contemporary Southern Africa.* Zed Books, 2006.

"Penang to Ban Foreign Cooks at Hawker Stalls in Bid to Safeguard Food Heritage." *Straits Times*, October 24, 2014. http://www.straitstimes.com/asia/se-asia/penang-to-ban-foreign-cooks-at-hawker-stalls-in-bid-to-safeguard-food-heritage.

Pérez, Efrén O. "Xenophobic Rhetoric and Its Political Effects on Immigrants and Their Co-Ethnics." *American Journal of Political Science* 59.3 (2015): 549–564.

Preston, Julia. "Immigrants Aren't Taking American's Jobs, New Study Finds." *New York Times*, September 21, 2016. https://www.nytimes.com/2016/09/22 /us/immigrants-arent-taking-americans-jobs-new -study-finds.html?mcubz=0&_r=0.

Reeves, Richard. *Infamy: The Shocking Story of the Japanese American Internment in World War II*. New York, NY: Henry Holt and Company, 2015.

Simpson, George Eaton, and J. Milton Yinger. *Racial and Cultural Minorities: An Analysis of Prejudice and Discrimination*. New York, NY: Springer Science & Business Media, 2013.

Southern African Migration Project. *The Perfect Storm: The Realities of Xenophobia in Contemporary South Africa*. No. 50. Inst for Democracy in South Africa, 2008.

Valencia, Nick. "My Encounter with Anti-Latino Racism." CNN, November 3, 2011. http://www.cnn.com /2011/09/29/opinion/valencia-racism-latino/index .html.

Wang, Amy B. "Portland Stabbing Victim's Last Words: 'Tell Everyone on This Train I Love Them.'" *Washington Post*, May 30, 2017. https://www.washingtonpost .com/news/post-nation/wp/2017/05/30/portland -stabbing-victims-last-words-tell-everyone-on-this -train-i-love-them/?utm_term=.e98293d84c25.

ABOUT THE AUTHOR

Susan Meyer is a writer and editor living and working in Austin, Texas, with her husband, Sam, and cat, Dinah. She is the author of numerous young adult nonfiction books. She supports the inclusion of all people in our diverse melting pot of a country. She enjoys attending cultural events in Austin and celebrating the many different cultures that make the city a rich and interesting place to live.

PHOTO CREDITS

Cover Hinterhaus Productions/Digital Vision/Getty Images; p. 5 Chandrajyoti Saikia/EyeEm/Getty Images; pp. 7, 17, 25, 26, 31, 43 Rawpixel.com/Shutterstock.com; p. 8 Ali Smith/Photodisc/Getty Images; p. 10 Lucky Business /Shutterstock.com; p. 12 ZUMA Press Inc/Alamy Stock Photo; p. 14 sirtravelalot/Shutterstock.com; p. 18 Vladimir Korostyshevskiy/Shutterstock.com; p. 20 Carl Mydans /The LIFE Picture Collection/Getty Images; p. 22 Rajesh Jantilal/AFP/Getty Images; p. 27 Barcin/E+/Getty Images; p. 30 Ababsolutum/E+/Getty Images; p. 32 Antonio Guillem/Shutterstock.com; p. 34 Monkey Business Images /Shutterstock.com; p. 37 Sipa USA via AP; pp. 38–39 Juanmonino/E+/Getty Images; p. 44 FPG/Archive Photos/Getty Images; pp. 46–47 iordani/Shutterstock.com; pp. 48–49 © iStockphoto.com/RoosterHD; pp. 52–53 Bloomberg/Getty Images.

Design: Michael Moy; Layout: Ellina Litmanovich; Editor: Amelie von Zumbusch; Photo Research: Karen Huang